Also by Gary Zukav

The Dancing Wu Li Masters
The Seat of the Soul

Reach for your soul. Reach even farther. The impulse of creation and power authentic—the hourglass point between energy and matter: that is the seat of the soul.

THOUGHTS FROM THE
SEAT
OF THE
SOUL

Meditations for Souls in Process

GARY ZUKAV

A FIRESIDE BOOK Published by Simon & Schuster New York London Toronto Sydney Tokyo Singapore

Rather than a soul in a body, become a body in a soul.

FIRESIDE
Rockefeller Center
1230 Avenue of the Americas
New York, New York 10020
Copyright © 1989, 1994 by Gary Zukav
All rights reserved
including the right of reproduction
in whole or in part in any form.
FIRESIDE and colophon are registered trademarks of Simon & Schuster Inc.
Designed by Bonni Leon
Manufactured in the United States of America
1 3 5 7 9 10 8 6 4 2

ISBN: 0-671-88769-6

Look at the probable futures that are unfolding before our world that is built upon the energy of the personality, and the probable futures that would unfold before a world that is built upon the energy of the soul. Which do you choose?

This book is dedicated to my sister,

Gail Zukav-Ross, who first requested it,

and whose friendship and love have

nurtured me for many years.

The final piece of reaching for authentic power is releasing your own to a higher form of wisdom.

FOREWORD

I hope that this book will be helpful to you as you move through the difficulties of your life as well as your joys. It is a special gift of love and appreciation. It has been designed to honor the pace of your growth. Its pages are not tied to the tyranny of a calendar. It is easy to read yet takes little space on your desk. Leave a thought showing for an afternoon, a day, or a week. Start at the beginning, or open to a place that draws you. Like Life, it

Release your specifications and say to the Universe: "Find me where you know I need to be." Let them go and trust that the Universe will provide, and so it shall.

is there for you with layers upon layers of depth and richness. How much you see depends only upon how much you allow yourself to open in the moment to the depth and richness of your own life.

This book is independent of *The Seat of the Soul*. If you have read *The Seat of the Soul*, you may enjoy having some thoughts from it available to you in this specially designed format. If thoughts that you encounter here are useful to you, you can explore them in detail in *The Seat of the Soul*.

In Love and Friendship,
Gary Zukav

We shall come to honor all of Life sooner or later. Our choices are when that shall happen, and the quality of experience that we shall have as we learn.

Are you comfortable with the thought that the Universe is alien and dead and no more than your five senses can detect? How does your heart respond to the thought that the Universe is alive and compassionate and that with it and with other souls of great power and Light you learn through the process of cocreating the reality that you experience?

The Universe backs the part of you that is of clearest intention.

We were taught that the organism that is best able to control both its environment and all of the other organisms in its environment is the most evolved. "Survival of the fittest." But our deeper understanding tells us that a truly evolved being is one that values others more than it values itself, and that values love more than it values the physical world and what is in it.

In a spiritual partnership you learn that wanting what you want is not enough, but that you must both want it deeply and create it every day, that you must bring it into being and hold it in being with your intentions.

While you are here you participate in the creation of both personal reality and impersonal reality. Just as you can participate in the creation of a building that will remain long after you are gone, you participate in the evolution of group energy dynamics that will remain after you are gone.

Behind every aspect of the health or illness of the body is the energy of the soul. It is the health of the soul that is the true purpose of the human experience. Everything serves that.

From the perception of the five-sensory human, we are alone in a universe that is physical. From the perception of the multisensory human, we are never alone, and the Universe is alive, conscious, intelligent and compassionate.

As you come to seek and see the virtues and strengths and nobilities of others, you begin to seek and see them in yourself also.

Every physical form, as well as every nonphysical form, is Light that has been shaped by consciousness. No form exists apart from consciousness.

By striving for a gold medal instead of a tin medal, or for prestige or notice, you ask the world to assess your value before you can value yourself. You place your sense of self worth in the hands of others. You have no power even if you win every gold medal that the world can produce.

You create your reality with your intentions.

Sometimes we speak of an afterlife, but we do not really believe that after we leave the Earth we are still responsible for the choices that we have made upon the Earth or our choices would be very different.

When we align our thoughts, emotions, and actions with the highest part of ourselves, we are filled with enthusiasm, purpose, and meaning. Life is rich and full. We have no thoughts of bitterness. We have no memory of fear. We are joyously and intimately engaged with our world. This is the experience of authentic power.

The loving personality seeks not to control, but to nurture, not to dominate, but to empower.

You are a dynamic being of Light that at each moment informs the energy that flows through you. You do this with each thought, with each intention.

Acompassionate heart is more effective against evil than an army. A compassionate heart can engage evil directly—it can bring Light where there was no Light.

A thought is energy, or Light, that has been shaped by consciousness.

Let go of what you think is just reward. Let go. Trust. Create. Be who you are. The rest is up to your nonphysical Teachers and the Universe.

From the perception of the five-sensory human, the physical world is an unaccountable given in which we unaccountably find ourselves, and we strive to dominate it so that we can survive. From the perception of the multisensory human, the physical world is a learning environment that is created jointly by the souls that share it, and everything that occurs within it serves their learning.

Choose with wisdom because the power is now fully in your hands.

Reverence is an attitude of honoring Life. You do not have to be authentically empowered to be gentle with Life or to love Life.

Are you not metaphorically within a Garden of Eden, your own creative reality, within which you choose each day how you will create with the male-female principle inside of you, the Adam and Eve principle? How will you use your power? Will you create Paradise or be Cast Out?

At each moment you choose the intentions that will shape your experiences and those things upon which you will focus your attention. If you choose unconsciously, you evolve unconsciously. If you choose consciously, you evolve consciously.

If your addiction lingers, ask yourself if you really want to release it, because in your heart you do not.

Choice is the engine of our evolution.

You gain or lose power according to the choices that you make.

The journey to authentic power requires that you become conscious of all that you feel.

The frequency of your Light depends upon your consciousness. When you shift the level of your consciousness, you shift the frequency of your Light.

Your soul is not a passive or a theoretical entity that occupies a space in the vicinity of your chest cavity. It is a positive, purposeful force at the core of your being. It is that part of you that understands the impersonal nature of the energy dynamics in which you are involved, that loves without restriction and accepts without judgment.

Trust the Universe. Trusting means that the circumstance that you are in is working toward your best and most appropriate end. There is no when to that. There is no if to that. It is.

The personality is those parts of the soul that require healing, along with those parts of the soul, such as compassion and love, that the soul has lent to the process of healing in that lifetime.

When the deepest part of you becomes engaged in what you are doing, when what you do serves both yourself and others, when you do not tire within but seek the sweet satisfaction of your life and your work, you are doing what you were meant to be doing.

We have formed our present understanding of evolution as a process of ever-increasing ability to dominate the environment and each other. This definition reflects the competition for external power that is generated by fear. Our deeper understanding leads us to a power that loves life in every form that it appears, a power that does not judge what it encounters, a power that perceives meaningfulness and purpose in the smallest details upon the Earth. This is authentic power.

The road to your soul is through your heart.

The true human condition in its most perfect form has no secrets. It does not hide, but exists in clear love.

When you feel in yourself the addictive attraction of sex, alcohol, drugs, or anything else, remember these words: You stand between the two worlds of your lesser self and your full self. Your lesser self is tempting and powerful because it is not as responsible or loving or disciplined, so it calls you. This other part of you is more responsible, caring, and empowered, but it demands of you the way of the enlightened spirit: conscious life. *Conscious* life. The other choice is unconscious permission to act without consciousness. It is tempting.

What choose you?

Being harmless means being so strong, so empowered, that the idea of showing power through harm is not even a part of your consciousness.

Temptation is the magnet which draws your awareness to that which would create negative karma if it were allowed to remain unconscious.

The club that kills can drive a stake into the ground to hold a shelter. The hands that build bombs can be used to build schools. The minds that coordinate the activities of violence can coordinate the activities of cooperation. When the activities of life are infused with reverence, they come alive with meaning and purpose.

Allow your intuition to guide your timing. Take it inside, ask how you feel, and then move forward.

Try to realize, and truly realize, that what stands between you and a different life are matters of responsible choice.

You are on a quest for authentic power. You cannot give up this quest. Your only choice is whether you wish to have the quest consciously or unconsciously.

Thoughts of vengeance, violence, and greed create emotions such as anger, hatred, jealousy, and fear and lower the frequency of your Light, or consciousness. Creative or loving thoughts invoke high-frequency emotions, such as appreciation, forgiveness and joy, and raise the frequency of your system.

Dwell in the company of your nonphysical Teachers and guides. Do not discriminate in terms of what you can and should ask and speak about. Just assume and live in the beauty of the bond. Do not fear dependency. What is wrong with being dependent upon the Universe?

Eventually, you will come to understand that love heals everything, and love is all there is.

Open yourself to your fellow humans. Allow yourself to experience what you feel toward them, and to hear what they feel. Your interactions with them form the basis of your growth.

We have come to view feelings as unnecessary appendages, like tonsils—useless, but capable of creating pain and dysfunction; but when we close the door to our feelings, we close the door to the vital currents that energize and activate our thoughts and actions.

It is not easy to express that which makes you feel vulnerable or painful or angry or upset. These are the emotions that empower words that can do either damage or can do so much healing.

Each decision that you make is an answer to the question, "How do you choose to learn love—through doubt and fear, or through wisdom?"

Keep your power just in the day that you are living on the Earth, and not on how to maneuver tomorrow.

Whether a person is reverent depends essentially upon whether he or she accepts the principle of the sacredness of Life, any way that he or she defines sacred.

If you decide that you cannot beat a temptation, what you are really doing is giving yourself permission to be irresponsible.

A nation is an aspect of the personality of Gaia, the Earth's soul, which, itself, is developing its personality and soul-hood.

Your parents are the souls to whom you are closest in your lifetime, and whose influence upon you is the greatest. Your soul and the souls of your parents agreed to your relationship in order to balance the energy that each needed to balance, or to activate dynamics within each other that are essential to lessons that each must learn.

Intuition is perception beyond the physical senses that is meant to assist you. It is that sensory system which operates without data from the five senses.

The path to reverence is through your heart, and only an awareness of your feelings can open your heart.

If you desire to know your soul, the first step is to recognize that you have a soul. The next step is to allow yourself to consider, "If I have a soul, what is my soul? What does my soul want? What is the relationship between my soul and me? How does my soul affect my life?"

In your moments of fear, recognize what your own power of choice is. You are not at the mercy of your inadequacy. The intention that will empower you must come from a place within you that suggests that you are indeed able to make responsible choices and draw power from them, that you are capable of acts of wholeness.

Sooner or later, each soul will turn toward authentic power. Every situation serves this goal, and every soul will reach it.

Before it incarnates, each soul enters into a sacred contract with the Universe to accomplish certain things. It enters into this commitment in the fullness of its being. Whatever the task that your soul has agreed to, all of the experiences of your life serve to awaken within you the memory of that contract, and to prepare you to fulfill it.

Where your attention goes, you go.

Your evolution toward authentic power affects not only you. As the quality of your consciousness reflects the clarity, humbleness, forgiveness and love of authentic power, it touches more and more around you.

Every action, thought, and feeling is motivated by an intention, and that intention is a cause that exists as one with an effect. If we participate in the cause, it is not possible for us not to participate in the effect. In this most profound way, we are held responsible for our every action, thought and feeling, which is to say, for our every intention.

Every intention sets energy into motion whether you are conscious of it or not. Each word that you speak carries consciousness—more than that, carries intelligence—and, therefore, is an intention that shapes Light.

You cannot begin the work of releasing an addiction until you can acknowledge that you are addicted.

Each choice that you make, to dwell in negativity or to take up residence in your heart, serves perfectly the evolution of your soul. All roads lead to home.

What is not learned in each lifetime is carried over into other lifetimes, along with new lessons that arise for the soul to learn, new karmic obligations that result from the responses of its personality to the situations that it encounters. The lessons that the soul has learned also are brought forward into other lifetimes, and this is how the soul evolves.

The place to begin the task of eliminating evil is within yourself.

What is behind your eyes holds more power than what is in front of them.

Pain by itself is merely pain, but the experience of pain coupled with an understanding that the pain serves a worthy purpose is suffering. Suffering can be endured because there is a reason for it that is worth the effort. What is more worthy of your pain than the evolution of your soul?

Feel your intentions in your heart. Feel not what your mind tells you, but what your heart tells you.

This is critical to understand: your addiction is not stronger than you. It is not stronger than who you want to be. Though it may feel that way, it can only win if you let it.

The perceptions of a multisensory human extend beyond physical reality to the larger dynamical systems of which our physical reality is a part. It is in this invisible realm that the origins of our deepest values are found, the motivations of those who consciously sacrifice their lives for higher purposes make sense, the power of Gandhi is explicable, and the compassionate acts of the Christ are comprehensible in a fullness that is not accessible to the five-sensory human.

You put your spiritual partnership most at risk by avoiding that which you are most afraid will destroy it.

It is not possible to understand your soul or your higher self or your intuition without coming to terms with the existence of nonphysical reality.

Power leaves you when you feel that the situation that you are in, or the people that you are with, do not command your respect.

Intuition is the voice of the nonphysical world.

Do not assume that the Universe operates like humankind, because it does not.

You give the Light of the Universe form. What you feel, what you think, how you behave, what you value and how you live your life reflect the way that you are shaping the Light that is flowing through you.

Nonphysical reality is your home. You came from nonphysical reality, you will return to nonphysical reality, and the larger part of you currently resides in, and evolves in, nonphysical reality.

The decisions that you make and the actions that you take upon the Earth are the means by which you evolve.

No matter how successful the personality becomes in accomplishing its goals, those goals will not be enough. Only when the personality begins to walk the path that its soul has chosen will it satisfy its hunger.

When a personality is in full balance, you cannot see where it ends and the soul begins. That is a whole human being.

As your temptations become greater, so does your ability to make responsible choices.

When fear ceases to scare you, it cannot stay.

It is wise to imagine the dynamics that we think of as "failure" and "success" as not truly existing, because they do not, not from the position of truth, only from the position of judgment.

An angry personality will respond to the difficulties of its life with anger, and thereby bring into being the necessity of experiencing the results of anger. A person who is angry, and yet reveres Life, however, will respond very differently to the difficulties of his or her life than a person who is angry and has no reverence for Life.

When you pray, you draw to you and invoke grace. Grace is uncontaminated conscious Light. Prayer brings grace and grace calms you. That is the cycle.

To experience relationships of substance and depth requires approaching and entering into relationships with consciousness and concern for the other.

You do what you do for yourself and your nonphysical Teachers and guides are there in assistance. They will never do it for you. It is not possible for them to do it for you. Delight in the dependency. Give your guides and Teachers permission to come closer.

Without commitment, you cannot learn to see others as your soul sees them—as beautiful and powerful spirits of Light.

You do not need to think that you create alone, but rather that you are guided strongly in ways to help cocreate in the most effective way for your healing and for the fulfillment of your contract.

Look at yourself as someone who is reaching for healing, and at the complexity of what needs to be healed. Do not think that you exist alone without other human beings of equal complexity.

Rather than serve the fake gods of your mind, serve your heart, the real God. You will not find God in your intellect. Divine Intelligence is in the heart.

Even into the toughest moments of your work on feelings of insecurity you can be light and remind yourself that you are spirits who have taken on the physical experience and have far greater power than you are showing in that moment of weakness.

When you feel that you are wanting what you do not have instead of what you do have, confront it. Realize that you are not in the present moment, you are not engaged in your present energy dynamic but, rather, you are letting energy leak to a future that does not exist.

Forgiveness means that you do not carry the baggage of an experience.

If you are not conscious of each part of yourself, you will have the experience of wanting to say one thing, and finding yourself saying something else. You will want your life to move in one direction, and find that it is moving in another. You will desire to release a painful pattern from your experience, and see it reappear yet again.

When energy leaves you in any way except in strength and trust, it cannot bring back to you anything but pain and discomfort. An authentically empowered human being, therefore, is a human being that does not release its energy except in love and trust.

Love is not a passive state. It is an active force. It is the force of the soul.

Compassion is being moved to and by acts of the heart.

Just as the many times human beings find themselves in circumstances where the hurt or the pain is so great that on their own power they cannot forgive, it is enough that they pray to be given the grace, the perception, the elevated Light that will allow them to forgive.

Recognition of your own addictions requires inner work. It requires that you look clearly at the places where you lose power in your life, where you are controlled by external circumstances. It requires going through your defenses.

By choosing your thoughts, and by selecting which emotional currents you will release and which you will reinforce, you determine the quality of your Light. You determine the effects that you will have upon others, and the nature of the experiences of your life.

Seeking out, facing with courage, and bringing into the light of consciousness that which is unconsciousness, and, therefore, in a position of power over the personality, is what heals.

If one person grieves at his or her experiences while another is able to laugh, who is the lighter? Who is harmless? The heart that dances is the innocent heart. It is the dancing heart that is harmless.

Nonphysical guidance is a partnership which challenges you to come to terms with the full width and breadth and depth of authentic power and responsible choice. It is not that you give permission to be mindlessly manipulated. It is that you give permission to be shown the fullest of your power and guided to its use.

The unearthing and healing of your negativities may appear to be an endless process, but it is not. Your vulnerabilities and weaknesses and fears are not different from those of your fellow humans. Do not despair because your humanness awakens.

If you do not like the relationship that you have with your husband or wife, and you would like it to be different, that desire alone will not change your relationship. That change begins with the intention to change it. How it will change depends upon the intention that you set.

Within a spiritual partnership you learn the roles of love and commitment and trust in making your partnership work. You learn that love alone is not enough—that without trust, you are not able to give and to receive the love that both of you have for each other.

Allow yourself to rest when you need it, to recognize when you become exhausted, and to know that even the best of us get tired.

Relax into the present moment.

Each personality draws to itself personalities with consciousness of like frequency, or like weakness. Therefore, the world of an angry person is filled with angry people, the world of a greedy person is filled with greedy people, and a loving person lives in a world of loving people.

It is impossible to create any action that does not have value. You may not see it, but that is irrelevant. Live in the trust that when it is appropriate, pieces will fall into place and you will see clearly.

Only through emotions can you encounter the force field of your own soul.

When you ask the Universe to bless you in your effort to align yourself with your soul, you open a passageway between yourself and your guides and Teachers. That is what a blessing is: the opening of a passageway between you and nonphysical guidance.

Think of what you are doing as entering into partnership with Divine Intelligence, a partnership in which you begin to share your concerns with the understanding that there is an Intelligence receptive to what you are saying that helps you create within your own environment of matter and energy the most effective dynamics to bring you into wholeness.

Awareness is a blissful state, not a painful one.

Take your hands off the steering wheel. Be able to say to the Universe, "Thy will be done," and to know it within your intentions.

What you are really feeling threatened by when you experience an artificial need is the loss of your power, and therefore, rather than being able to address it directly, you create an artificial need that does the speaking for you. Learn to address the real need so that you do not have to burden yourself with behavioral patterns that give you some artificial persona that you have to live up to.

Knowledge is power, and for each level of knowledge, you are held responsible for how you use it.

In order to make a responsible choice you must ask yourself, "What will this produce? Do I really want to create that? Am I ready to accept all of the consequences of this choice?"

Clarity is the perception of wisdom and the ability to see the soul in action in the physical world. It turns pain into suffering and evaporates fear. Clarity allows you to see the world of physical matter for what it is, a learning environment that is created jointly by the intentions of the souls that share it.

Evil needs to be understood for what it is: the dynamic of the absence of Light. It is not something that one should prepare to battle, to run from or to outlaw.

Reverence is simply the experience of accepting that all Life is, in and of itself, of value.

When you do kindly things to yourself then you know what it is to be able to love yourself.

Each time you feel negative, stop, acknowledge that you are, and discharge it consciously. Ask what you are feeling and what is at the root of it. Go for the root of it in that instant and as you work to pull the root, simultaneously look at the positive side and remind yourself of the greater truth that there is something spiritually profound at work, that your life is no accident, that you are under contract.

When you release a negative thought, or a negative feeling, you release lower-frequency currents of energy from your system, and this, literally, allows an increase in the frequency of your consciousness.

The choice not to choose is the choice to remain unconscious and, therefore, to wield power irresponsibly.

A person who seeks relationships only to gratify his or her own needs, such as his or her own emotional or sexual needs, will find that each relationship is essentially identical, that the people in his or her life are replaceable, that experiences with the first and experiences with the second are essentially the same.

The loss of a mate, or a friend, or a colleague through distrust is not a punishment for distrustfulness. It is the result of refusing to look consciously within oneself at the issue of trust.

Authentic needs are the needs that are always met by the Universe.

The multisensory personality is more radiant and energetic than the five-sensory personality. It is aware of the Light of its soul, and it is able to detect, and to communicate with, forms of Life that are invisible to the five-sensory personality.

When you ask for guidance and assistance, simply assume that it immediately is pouring forward. You may need to have lunch, or drive into town or do whatever it is that you need to do in order to relax your mind to hear or to feel, but live in the total assumption that the moment that you ask for guidance it is pouring in.

Every circumstance and situation gives you the opportunity to choose to allow your soul to shine through you, to bring into the physical world through you its unending and unfathomable reverence for and love of Life.

To live with reverence means being willing to say, "That is Life, we must not harm it," and "Those are our fellow humans, we must not destroy them," and mean it.

What is in one is in the whole, and therefore, ultimately, each soul is responsible for the whole world.

What we think of as physical reality is an intermingling of appropriate realities, a fluid massive consciousness in which each of us exists independently of each other and yet co-exists interdependently with each other.

All souls are tempted, but an individual with limitations of consciousness will find it more attractive to walk into the magnetic field of fear because it would not recognize fear for what it is. It would accept it as something else, as something that is normal to Life.

The type of power that you are trying to transform in yourself is the type of power that needs to be transformed in general upon the Earth.

The illusion for each soul is created by its intentions. Therefore, the illusion is alive at each moment with the most appropriate experiences that you can have in order for your soul to heal.

When the personality comes fully to serve the energy of its soul, that is authentic empowerment. This is the goal of the evolutionary process in which we are involved and the reason for our being.

Temptation is that dynamic through which each soul is graciously offered the opportunity to learn without creating karma, to evolve directly through conscious choice.

When you commit to a spiritual partnership with another human being, you begin to see that what is necessary to the health of your partnership is identical with what is necessary to your own spiritual growth, that each of you holds the pieces that the other is missing.

The way of the heart is one of compassion and emotional perception.

The perception that someone else is responsible for what you experience underlies the idea that forgiveness is something that one person does for another. How can you forgive another person for the fact that you have chosen to step out of your power?

Answers that come through your intuition may challenge what you would prefer to do. Your lower self, your personality, will not challenge, but rationalize.

It is impossible to have a prayer without power.

The personality resists acknowledging its addictions because that forces it to choose to leave a part of itself out of control, or to do something about it. Once an addiction has been acknowledged, it cannot be ignored, and it cannot be released without changing your life, your self-image, and your entire perceptual and conceptual framework.

Trust allows you to follow your feelings through your defenses to their sources, and to bring to the light of consciousness those aspects of yourself that resist wholeness, that live in fear.

Do not lose power over the what-ifs of your life. These are unlimited and endless. Keep your power in the now, in present time.

The challenge, and the task, for the advanced or expanding mind is to expand to a level at which questions that cannot be answered from within the accepted understanding of truth can be answered.

Consider how powerful the soul is if it can have a part of itself that experiences great love, a part of itself that experiences fears, a part that is perhaps neutral, a part that experiences schizophrenia, and a part that is dramatically compassionate.

How do you know what "success" is? Can you see in fullness the causes and effects of your being and of your acts and of your words? Therefore, how do you know what success is, and how can you possibly imagine what failure is?

Ajoyous person abounds with energy and feels buoyant, because he or she is running a higher-frequency current of energy through his or her system.

Be mindful of the words that you use and the actions that you live and who you are and how it is you use your power. Keep clear at all times that you are what you say you are.

We need truth to grow in the same way that we need vitamins, affection and love.

Loving others, or how you treat yourself, is really your own dose of your own medicine that you give to others at the same time.

Every time you ask for guidance, you receive it. Every time you ask yourself, "What is my motivation?," you ask the Universe, "Help me to see," and help comes.

The archetype of spiritual partnership reflects the conscious journey of multisensory humans toward authentic power. Spiritual partners consciously cocreate their experiences with each other, with an alive Earth that loves Life very much, and with a compassionate Universe.

It is not until you have the courage to engage in human relationships that you grow.

You can just as easily laugh and play while you grow as become serious and overwhelmed.

Spiritual partnership is a sacred commitment between the partners to assist each other's spiritual growth. Spiritual partners recognize their equality.

Although what you encounter and what you do in each moment is appropriate and perfect to the evolution of your soul, the shape of the experiences of your life is determined nonetheless by the choices that you make. It is you that chooses to linger in resentment, or to be consumed by anger, or enveloped in grief, or to release these lower-frequency currents of energy.

You are always being given opportunities to love and be loved, yet ask yourself how many times in your life you have squandered these opportunities.

The part of yourself that reaches toward Light may not be the strongest part of you at the moment that you choose to journey toward authentic power, but it is the part that the Universe backs.

When you choose not to forgive, the experience that you do not forgive sticks with you.

The great soul is the person who has taken on the task of change. If he or she is able to transcend fear, to act out of courage, the whole of its group will benefit and each one, in his or her own life, will be suddenly more courageous, though they may not see how or why.

An intention is a quality of consciousness that you bring to an action.

When you choose to learn through wisdom, to evolve consciously, your fears surface one at a time in order for you to exorcise them with inner faith. That is how it happens. You exorcise your own demons.

When you choose to respond to life's difficulties with compassion and love instead of fear and doubt, you create a "heaven on Earth"—you bring the aspects of a more balanced and harmonious level of reality into physical being.

Sexual addictions are the most universal within our species because the issues of power are tied so directly to the learning of sexuality within the human structure. A person cannot be in his or her own power center and be sexually out of control or dominated by the sexual energy current. These cannot exist simultaneously.

The personality emerges as a natural force from the soul. It is an energy tool that the soul adapts to function within the physical world. Each personality is unique because the configuration of energy of the soul that formed it is unique.

Forgiveness means that you do not hold others responsible for your experiences. If you do not hold yourself accountable, and if you are not satisfied with what you experience, you will seek to change it by manipulating another.

No two people have the same reality.

You do not stop losing power by refusing to recognize your fear, by anesthetizing yourself to what you feel. The road to authentic power is always through what you feel through your heart.

When seen through authentically empowered eyes, a being with a higher rank in creation is one that has more ability to see without obstruction, more ability to live in love and wisdom, and more ability and desire to help others evolve into the same love and Light.

There would be no accumulation of strength inside if the choices that you make did not require discipline and intention.

When you consciously invoke growing, you consciously invoke the parts of yourself that are not whole to come into the foreground of your life. With each recurrence of anger, jealousy, or fear, you are given the choice to challenge it, or to give in to it. Each time you challenge it, it loses power and you gain power.

When you align yourself with your personality, you give power to external circumstances and objects. You disempower yourself. As you grow aware of your spiritual self and your origin, your immortalness, and you choose according to that first and the physical second, you close the gap that exists between the personality and the soul. You begin to experience authentic power.

The challenge to each human is creation. Will you create with reverence, or with neglect?

The difference between a great soul that aligns itself with openness and growth and interdependence, that transcends its fear on behalf of itself and its collective, and one that does not is that the soul that chooses openness has a different active level of courage and insight and wisdom, and the one that does not has consistently weakened under the impact of the fear of the collective.

The physical reality of the Earth school is shaped by the decisions of those who are in it.

It is not necessary to learn what we need to learn and have it cost somebody his or her life. It is not necessary for the experience of progress to cost the destruction of nature. It is not necessary, but without a sense of reverence for Life, who cares that it destroys Life?

There is no single optimal path for the soul. There are many optimal paths. With each choice you immediately create numerous paths within a choice, one of which is then optimal.

Your intentions create the reality that you experience. Until you become aware of this, it happens unconsciously. Therefore, be mindful of what you project. That is the first step toward authentic power.

Try looking at life as a beautifully well-organized dynamic.

Love is the energy of the soul. Love is what heals the personality. There is nothing that cannot be healed by love. There is nothing but love.

What makes a spiritual, or sacred, partnership is that the souls within the partnership understand that they are together in a committed relationship, but the commitment is not to physical security. It is rather to be with each other's physical lives as they reflect spiritual consciousness.

It is emotionally, spiritually impossible to have a sexual connection with a human being and not ignite certain emotional patterns, but they are a continual dead-end street when there is no relationship or true emotional feelings to go with the act.

When you seek to dominate another you dominate no one but disempower yourself.

Temptation is a dress rehearsal for a karmic experience of negativity.

At each instant you make decisions in the form of your attitudes about the Universe, about other people, and about yourself and your experiences at each moment are created by them.

The pains that you suffer, the lonelinesses that you encounter, the experiences that are disappointing or distressing, the addictions and seeming pitfalls of your life are each doorways to awareness. Each offers you an opportunity to see beyond the illusion that serves the balancing and growth of your soul.

It is impossible for you to come full circle in this way of empowerment without prayer. Be able to say within your intentions and your meditations, "And I ask for guidance or help," and expect to get it. Expect to get it.

Taking into account the consequences of your decisions is responsible choice.

The soul is. It has no beginning and no end but flows toward wholeness.

If we perceived Life with reverence, we would stand in awe at the experience of physical Life and walk the Earth in a very deep sense of gratitude.

You are related to every form of Life upon this planet and beyond. As your soul evolves, you move into greater awareness of the nature of that relationship, and the responsibilities that you assume.

Your consciousness affects every cell in your body, and every cell in your body affects your consciousness.

Reverence is engaging in a form and a depth of contact with Life that is well beyond the shell of form and into essence.

Move into how strong the power of your addiction is, and ask yourself if the time is really right for you to release this form of learning. That is for you to ask and answer.

The creation of physical experience through intention, the infusion of Light into form, energy into matter, soul into body, are all the same.

No being, not even a nonphysical Teacher, can assume responsibility for your life, for the way that you choose to use your energy, but a nonphysical Teacher can help you to understand what your choices and your experiences represent. It can provide you with the knowledge to choose responsibly, and hopefully, choose wisely.

By keeping your emotions clear, emotional negativity does not reside in you, and you become lighter and lighter. This opens your intuitive track because it allows you a clear sense of loving.

Anything that creates or increases a sense of separation within a person shatters the soul or in some form diminishes its strength, not to be confused with its immortality.

From the perception of the five-sensory human, intentions have no effects, the effects of actions are physical, and not all actions affect us or others. From the perception of the multisensory human, the intention behind an action determines its effects, every intention affects both us and others, and the effects of intentions extend far beyond the physical world.

When you assume responsibility for what you experience and share what you experience in a spirit of companionship, that is the same as forgiveness. When you hold someone responsible for what you experience, you lose power.

Do not insist that the Universe comply with your understanding of it.

As you give so it shall be given to you. If you give with judgment, limitation and stinginess, that is what you will create in your life. If you radiate love and compassion, you do receive it.

To incarnate, the soul creates a personality from those parts of itself that it wants to heal in the physical environment, and from those parts that it lends to the process of healing in that lifetime. Therefore, you can see within a person's personality the splintered suffering of the soul from which it is formed, as well as the grace that the soul has earned, which is the loving part of the personality.

Y_{ou} cannot not evolve. Everything in the Universe evolves. It is only a question of which way you will choose to learn as you evolve. This is always your choice, and there is always wisdom in each choice.

In order to release your addiction, it is necessary to enter your inadequacies, to recognize that they are real, and to bring them into the light of consciousness to heal.

When you understand that the experiences of your life are necessary to the balancing of the energy of your soul, you are free to not react to them personally, to not create more negative karma for your soul.

It is not enough to want or to intend or to meditate. You must pray. You must talk to the Universe. You must ask. You must believe. That is partnership.

When the personality, Jesus, encountered the Luciferic principle, the challenging dynamic of the human experience—when he was offered dominion over the entire globe—was he tempted? Yes, he was tempted. If he were not, there would have been no power in his choice. Authentic empowerment is not gained by making choices that do not stretch you.

As you discharge negative energy consciously and set your intentions according to what your heart tells you, you move toward becoming a being of the Light, fully whole and empowered and inwardly secure, and you draw to yourself the Universe's greatest gift: human beings with open hearts.

It is never appropriate to suppress an emotion, or to disregard what you feel. If you do not know what you feel, you cannot come to know the splintered nature of your personality, and to challenge those aspects and those energies that do not serve your development.

Your choice comes in knowing appropriate timing, clear motivation, and trust.

If you strike without compassion against the darkness, you yourself enter the darkness.

Nonjudgmental justice is the freedom of seeing what you see and experiencing what you experience without responding negatively. It relieves you of the self-appointed job of judge and jury because you know that everything is being seen—nothing escapes the law of karma—and this brings forth understanding and compassion.

There is a difference between personal truth and impersonal truth. They are both truth, but personal truth is yours, and impersonal truth belongs to all that is, to each person.

Consider that the ocean is God. It has always been. Now reach in and grab a cup full of water. In that instant, the cup becomes individual, but it has always been, has it not? This is the case with your soul.

Grace is the tranquilizer of the soul. With grace comes a knowing that what you are experiencing is necessary. It calms you with a sense of knowing.

Knowing in the cognitive sense cannot produce proof of nonphysical reality any more than it can produce proof of God.

Do not suffer in aloneness. There is no such thing.

The higher order of logic and understanding that is capable of reflecting the soul comes from the heart.

If the soul experiences an absence of Light from a part of itself, the personality will experience this absence of Light as fear. That fear is of the personality, and, therefore, of space and time. Unconditional love is of the soul, instantaneous, Universal, not bound.

If you have conflicting intentions, different dynamics will be set in motion and oppose each other. If you are not aware of all of your intentions, the strongest one will win. If your personality is whole, the Light that flows through it is focused into a single, clear beam, and your intentions are powerful and effective.

The heart of making a temptation that is greater than you can resist is that you do not wish to be held responsible for your choice.

Allow yourself to experience what it is to learn step by step the freedom that comes from being unattached to the outcome, but operating from an empowered heart.

How is it possible to know what to pursue within the illusion and what not to pursue? Ask yourself what are your genuine needs, and what are the needs that you have created to control or maneuver others, or to gain attention?

As you choose to empower yourself, the temptation that you challenge will surface again and again. Each time that you challenge it, you gain power and it loses power.

The perception of power as external that separates nations is the same that exists between individuals; and the love, clarity and compassion that emerge within the individual that chooses consciously to align itself with its soul is the same that will bring sexes, races, nations and neighbors into harmony with each other.

Do what you need to do in the present moment. Yours is not to worry about that which we call the future.

The process of destroying Life while we are learning about Life that has characterized our evolution would cease, or at least would be very different if we approached Life with a quality of reverence.

As you acquire a sense of reverence, you develop a capacity to think more deeply about the value of Life before you commit your energy to action. When you are fully reverent, you cannot harm Life, even if you are unempowered.

Give yourself permission to choose the most positive behavior in each moment.

If you are unkind to yourself you will be unkind to others, and if you are negligent of yourself you will be that to others. Only by feeling compassion for yourself can you feel compassion for others.

If you are unaware of your intention, or if you suspect that you are operating from a second agenda, ask yourself, "What is really going on?" Check your motivation. That automatically engages guidance. You will not be alone in your assessment.

It may be that your addiction has provided you one of the few genuine pleasures of your life. What is more important to you, your wholeness and your freedom, or the pleasures that you get from satisfying your addiction?

If you wish the world to become loving and compassionate, become loving and compassionate yourself. If you wish to diminish fear in the world, diminish your own. These are the gifts that you can give.

The illusion holds power over you when you are not able to remember that you are a powerful spirit that has taken on the physical experience for the purpose of learning.

Your struggles themselves do not create karma or determine the way that you will evolve, only your responses to them.

Spiritual partners commit to a growing dynamic. Their commitment is truly a promise toward their own growth, to their own spiritual survival and enhancement, and not to their physical.

Until you become aware of the effects of your anger, you continue to be an angry person.

By becoming the other person, by truly walking into the fears of the other and then returning into your own being again, you open up the conversation to transcend the personal and become impersonal.

When you choose the energy of your soul—creating with the intentions of love, forgiveness, humbleness and clarity—you gain power. When you choose to learn through wisdom, you gain power. When you choose to create with the energy of your personality—with anger, jealousy, or fear—you lose power.

As a personality becomes multisensory, its intentions—its hunches and subtle feelings—become important to it. It comes to recognize intentions, and to respond to them rather than to the actions and the words that it encounters. It can recognize, for example, a warm heart beneath a harsh and angry manner, and a cold heart beneath polished and pleasing words.

When an individual invokes the energy of the archetype of spiritual partnership, not only the partnership that it forms with another individual is affected, but also its community, nation and the global village. It is not just you that is evolving through your decisions, but the entirety of humanity.

With each choice that you make to align yourself with the energy of your soul, you empower yourself. Authentic power is built up step by step, choice by choice. It cannot be meditated or prayed into being. It must be earned.

No question is unheard, and no question goes unanswered. "Ask and you shall receive" is the rule, but you must learn how to ask and how to receive.

Without an awareness of our feelings we cannot experience compassion. How can we share the sufferings and the joys of others if we cannot experience our own?

Within each experience of pain or negativity is the opportunity to challenge the perception that lies behind it and to choose to learn with wisdom.

Prayer is moving into a personal relationship with Divine Intelligence.

Nonjudgmental justice does not judge the process of the soul's evolution except that it recognizes with love that the soul is reaching for love.

If you choose to forgive someone who has wronged you rather than to hate that person, you shift the frequency of your Light.

It is possible to respect one person and not respect another, but it is not possible to revere one person without revering every person.

Hatred of evil does not diminish evil, it increases it.

When you fear that your ability to love or to be loved is threatened, you experience physical discomfort or pain near your heart. What we experience, literally, as heartache is the experience of power leaving in fear or distrust through this energy center.

When we experience fear or anger or jealousy, we are in an illusion that is designed to bring to awareness those parts of the soul that require healing. These things do not actually exist. That is why pursuing them does not bring power. What exists between souls is love, and that is all that exists.

You cannot, and will not, encounter a circumstance, or a single moment, that does not serve directly and immediately the need of your soul to heal, to come into wholeness.

Humble spirits are free to love and to be who they are. They have no artificial standards to live up to.

A responsible choice is a choice that takes into account the consequences of each of your choices.

Whether an interaction between souls is healing or not depends upon whether the personality involved can see beyond itself and that of the other personality to the interaction of their souls. This perception automatically draws forth compassion.

Truth is that which does not contaminate you, but empowers you. Therefore, there are degrees of truth, but, generically, truth is that which can do no harm. It cannot harm.

Morality is a human creation. The Universe does not judge.

By remaining in your power you do not become a static energy system, one that hoards energy to itself. You become a stable energy system, capable of conscious acts of focus and intention. You become a magnet for those who are illumined and those who want to be.

Just as you dispose of your physical body's wastes and toxins, so, too, dispose of your emotional wastes and toxins by finishing emotionally unfinished business, by not going to bed in anger, by seeing that you do not feel contaminated emotionally, and by learning to work with and to honor your emotional currents of energy.

Behind fear is powerlessness.

As the anger or fear within a personality builds, the world in which it lives increasingly reflects the anger or fear that it must heal, so that eventually, the personality will see that it is creating its own experiences and perceptions, that its righteous anger or justifiable fear originates within itself, and therefore can be replaced by other perceptions and experiences only through the force of its own being.

The human emotional system can be broken down into roughly two elements: fear and love. Love is of the soul. Fear is of the personality.

If you are not conscious of all of the different parts of yourself, the part of yourself that is the strongest will win out over the other parts. Its intention will be the one that the personality uses to create its reality.

The greater the desire of your soul to heal your addiction, the greater will be the cost of keeping it.